The DAY SHE LEARNED *To* SPEAK

The DAY SHE LEARNED *To* SPEAK

Nicole Leva

gatekeeper press
Columbus, Ohio

This book is a work of fiction. The names, characters, and events in this book are the products of the author's imagination or are used fictitiously. Any similarity to real persons living or dead is coincidental and not intended by the author.

The views and opinions expressed in this book are solely those of the author and do not necessarily reflect the views or opinions of Gatekeeper Press. Gatekeeper Press is not to be held responsible for and expressly disclaims responsibility of the content herein.

THE DAY SHE LEARNED TO SPEAK

Published by **Gatekeeper Press**
2167 Stringtown Rd, Suite 109
Columbus, OH 43123-2989
www.GatekeeperPress.com

Copyright © 2022 by **Nicole Leva**

Illustrations by **Arianna Justiniano**

All rights reserved. Neither this book, nor any parts within it may be sold or reproduced in any form or by any electronic or mechanical means, including information storage and retrieval systems, without permission in writing from the author. The only exception is by a reviewer, who may quote short excerpts in a review.

The cover design for this book is entirely the product of the author. Gatekeeper Press did not participate in and is not responsible for any aspect of this element.

Library of Congress Control Number: 2022931477

ISBN (paperback): 9781662925252

For Mom,

The strongest love I've ever known

The day she learned to speak
Was really unlike any other
Maybe she had finally had enough
She hit her breaking point
She stopped bending and started to snap
That spark that was always inside her
Lit into a roaring flame that would never
be extinguished again
Out of her mouth sprung hordes of wildflowers
Roses with sharp thorns bloomed between her lips
They made her bleed as she spoke the first words
She roared her hurt
She howled her truth
She sung her sad memories
And she whispered her deep love
She had begun to bloom
And she would never be cut down
She would never look back

Men fell for her flawless beauty
Dropped to their knees, looking into her topaz eyes
Wanting to run their hands through her untamed curls
They shot at her like arrows
Lyrical poetry straight from their poisoned mouths
But men are all the same
She knew this
They wanted to conquer her
Control her
After taking what they wanted she would be
locked in a garden
Pretty to look at but never truly free
Driven by their desires
The men tried to capture her but they always forgot
To watch out for her thorns
For she was a wild rose

Do not let them tell you
Kindness is a weakness
My dear, they are all terrified
For as they morph into ugly monsters
You stay beautifully human

Dear Girls,
The way you miss red flags
The rules
The obsessions
The raised hands
The countless lies
Is with open hearts
But closed eyes

I left town to go find myself
But the farther I went
The more pieces started to fall
I let each boy take and take
Until I was a jagged shard
Instead of a girl whole
I only found
How to lose my fucking soul

My mind holds fevered dreams as of late
I toss and turn all night
Unable to escape
I dream my mouth is open
I can't scream and emit no sound
In another dream
My life is a ship sinking and I am bound
and ready to drown
Tonight I am fighting for my life
And it actually becomes a good dream
No longer bad and scary
For tonight I yell and holler
I whip my arms and swing my fists
Tonight
I stand a chance

Sink your teeth into empowering yourself
Instead of devouring yourself

*

If you let rose colored glasses decide your fate
You won't see the thorns until it's too late

*

My God, if only you could see
You are so much more then society tells you to be

And I wonder if eyes will ever see
as deeply as the heart feels
And if the mouth could ever sing
the music a soul makes

The strongest armor
Known to mankind
Is
A
Woman's
Mind

Men can spin a tale of lies
Faster than any spider and its web
Maybe that's why I feel so inclined
To always stomp arachnids dead

To say you mean the world to me
Is a dirty lie
I can't encompass your being
To one lowly planet
When above our skies
Are shooting stars
And firework novas
Milky ways made from daring dreams
You aren't the world to me
You are a galaxy

They say if you love someone
You should accept their flaws
But I don't think that's true
Maybe the flaws that are a part of you
Are the missing pieces of me too
I knew it wouldn't be easy
I asked for a journey
Maybe our love is an adventure
And the flaws are mountains
Together we climb
Maybe that's what it means
For me to be yours
And you to be mine

It was all so raw
As if I had been in some great battle
And was all bloodied
Yet I didn't bear a single scratch
It was all on the inside
I felt as if I had received some fatal wound
that I couldn't recover from
There was no healing from this
My ribs tore from my chest
Showing the world my broken and battered heart
My God, it was so ugly
This is all I had left to give
My bruised pride
My uneven smile that never lasted
I tried to make it straight but it was forced
And pretty soon it fell off my face completely
All my tears that made even the ocean look small ran
forever and choked me
I tried to run and hide but I couldn't curl up
into a small enough ball
I was so so raw

She wrote
Of heartaches and heartbreaks
Like a poisoned apple she bit
From her pen the black ink dripped

She wrote
Of the innocence in believing in true love
This ironically
Led her to create her sins

But as she wrote
It started to rain
Slowly, very slowly
It washed away the pain

Rumors fly

Lovers lie

The world goes round

It spins and spins

Like my brain in my head

Every time I overthink as I stand looking over the brink

I might just jump off the edge

*

She broke the dawn with her smile
Because she survived another day
In this society
With its deadly mind games

24 ...　　　THE DAY SHE LEARNED TO SPEAK

She prefers a cactus over flowers
They don't just wilt and die
They are survivors

As women we are taught to be selfless
I wish someone would've shook our shoulders
And taught us more important things
Like it's okay to put yourself first
Like it's okay to be selfish

Warrior

Wild

Winner

Wisdom

Woman

It's no coincidence

Our creator knew what made perfect sense

I smell rain on the horizon
Carried swiftly by the winds
And I wonder
Is it here to cleanse all my sins?

Fight the impossible
Punch the air even when you tire of blows
Howl back at the wind until you can't speak
Claw at the dirt until your nails break
Stand tall
Don't shrink against the thunder and lightning
With the rain pouring down, threatening to drown you
Run as hard as you can
Mother Nature won't scare you
Once you've been beaten by a man

Her eyes are deep lagoons
Of earthy browns
Interlaced with specks of mystery
And filled to the brim
With emotional history

I am in a constant state of
Wanting to be needed
And needing to be left the fuck alone

"She was never the same"
No, she wasn't
She stopped being the girl who waited for a knight in shining armor
Her mind twisted to match a sinner's attitude
Her sweet mouth started spitting venom
She tore down that measly wall he had so easily climbed
And rebuilt a new one better matched with her rage
This one made of burning fire

※

How do you lift a fallen star
Back to the sky
And explain to them that they can't shine
Without a little darkness?

They never fail to ask, mystified
As they dig their claws into my past
"What was the hardest part?
The swimming across the ocean or the fateful dive?"
I'd like to rake my claws across their faces
The ones whose deepest journeys were through pitiful puddles
I smile sweetly instead
Look them all in the eye
"It was after I drowned, the coming back to life"

Broken bones hurt like a bitch
But broken hearts even more
Trust me
I've shattered both before

I pace in the dark
Back and forth and back again
Confined to these bars and my thoughts
My captor lurking in the shadows
I know she's here
If only she would come close
I would reach my hands through these small gaps

I hiss "Come near"
Silence; it's always silent
No, sometimes she laughs
They all laugh at me echoing off barren walls
They think I'm a pet locked up in this black birdcage
If only they knew how much this fuels my rage

The velvet pillows underneath me
Do little to give me comfort
They are good at soaking up my tears however
Who knew it would be so plush at rock bottom?
Where I am held prisoner forever

There is but one window
Dirt-streaked and grimy
After it rains sometimes the light shines through, it beams down
Bringing her from the shadows
Until we are eye to eye

I gnash my teeth, scrape my claws
Against these prison bars
She creeps close as I demand from her
The key
Lifting her hood, she shakes her head, pointing at me

Shock
I stare upon my own face
Hair in knots, dark circles under my eyes
I am her—no, she is I?
A trick
It's a silver sheen casting this show

The mirror talks with my own mouth
"Let me go"
Our eyes widen
My hand and hers reach for the walls of bars
at the same time
Easily we open this gilded cage of mine
It was never locked

"I don't understand" we utter at the same time
"You didn't lock me inside?"
"No" we both reply
"You've just been stuck inside your own mind"

Eventually the girl lost all hope
There were strings attached to her happiness
And fate knew how to pull and twist them into a tangle
It was as if the trickster god watched her
So she begged to be unseen
Because every time she dared to dream
To wish upon a star
the best giver of false hope
Every time she gave in to her damn bleeding heart
Like clockwork everything fell apart

Dear young souls,
Someone should tell you
That there are things you will have to learn on your own
How to pull a knife out of your back
How to cry silently when everyone else is asleep
When it's time to stop begging for another's attention
Why you can't catch your breath when you're in love
(And also when you fall out of it)
But the most important thing
Is to learn your self-worth
I'm not talking about value
I'm talking about the depth of your existence
You need to learn
That your imagination can run wild
Your mouth can speak volumes
Your body is a temple that you choose to decorate
however you desire
And if anyone and I mean anyone tries to ruin that for you
You may also learn
That you are allowed to take those bridges
And let them burn

I rolled my dice
Letting the wind take all my lucky chances
Making me dance
Like leaves in fall

They say God only gives you as much as you can handle
He plucks me out of my peaceful life
And drops me in the ocean with no hesitation
"Drown" he says
And every time
Every damn time I crawl back onto shore
Salt water in my lungs and sand in my throat
He looks down smiling at me
But when I look up
I notice that smile never fully reaches
His eyes

Even with all the words left unsaid
I heard you
On your quietest days I paid the most attention
I took your emotions tenfold into myself
I pushed my ache down until it found a tear and started to leak
When I wept out loud
You simply dismissed me
What a fool I was
To think you would love me differently

✷

As the moon glows in her full form
I can't help but envy
The magical pull she has to draw all those eyes
From all around the world
Onto her
Only her

Woven into the palms of my hand lie
Burnt stars I've already reached for
I think I will use them as bait
When night falls and I hear the fevered call
Of dreams just past my grasp
For now

Let us lay in a puddle of our emotions
Let there be tears
Screams
Laughter
Wishes
And pleas
Let there be no sound and all sound
We don't have to touch
We can just finally be allowed to feel

I want to sink
Dive
Burrow
Into my thoughts and dreams
No, I don't need any light
Don't touch me
Kindly shut up
And just let me think

I went searching for answers
I spent time digging for truths
Drew a couple maps
Even built a ship or two
I wasted so much time losing myself
While I was looking for you

The most beautiful souls are hidden away
Those invisible walls are like caverns
You have to dig deep
And you can't always see where you're going
In the dark you will question everything
Do they know you are there?
Do they even care?
But I beg you
Keep digging
Because what they are
Is the rarest gem
Brighter than any star

*

Keeping you afloat
Is drowning me

Once again she drowned in her tears
Knowing the ocean would never be one of her fears

*

My heart hurts
It sears my soul with the pain of loving another
But that's okay
I'll carve these feelings deep in my being
Like a fresh bleeding tattoo
I'll wear these scars with pride
It's a daily reminder I need to feel
To remember no matter what
I will survive

The audacity of begging for forgiveness
when you aren't even sorry
What a mystery
No
The fucking audacity

What happened to you?
Is it time that causes damage?
Or did I never truly know the real you?
So many questions unanswered
But the truth would probably hurt more
So I close the door on our love and future
Still, I won't rest until I know
When did you lose your soul?

"I won't text you again"
There's a kind of finality to it, isn't there?
When you said it out loud it was okay
When you forced yourself to not answer you survived
But when he says the words
It's like someone hit a panic button
This is it
You convinced yourself you had given up long ago
That you were done
But now he's done
And some deep buried hope inside your chest
Is threatening to burst
This is your last chance
We can fix this
Fix what?
Picking up the broken shards
Will only hurt you further
You don't play with glass
So you delete the final message
You turn off your phone
You shut Pandora's box

It wasn't until I was deep
Within pages and ink
That I found the words
I was always afraid to say out loud

I found

Our heartbeats matched each other's

When we sat with the simplicity of no sound

Hurt me

Backstab me

Break me

Slap me

Yell at me

Shake me

Hate me

Love me

Caress me

Take me

Kiss me

Walk with me

Talk with me

Look at me

Touch me

But you will never be what created me

That was and always will be me

There is a special crime for those who break hearts
They are cursed to walk 100 years amongst a beach with sharp glass for sand
And as their soles bleed and they cry and weep
I shall descend from the sea and tell them there is a way to escape
Put the shards back together until they are whole again
They will try and fail and cry and beg
Claiming they cannot fix this sand of glass
And the truth will pour in with the tide
This is not glass
But pieces of broken hearts
And no, you cannot put it back together again
You cannot make it as it once was
Whole and untarnished with no cracks or sharp edges
You cannot simply glue back together a broken heart
You cannot stop the hurt once it has begun to start
And maybe they will learn their lesson
Never shatter another's heart again

✻

The greatest lie told in the history of ever
Is that you were only born to love another

*

They never let you feel anymore
They never let you grieve
"You will be okay"
"You will get through this"
"You are strong"
"It's better you found out now"
Just let me cry my tears
Just let my anger howl

Every time I look, that silver sheen seems to crack
Replicating a broken soul staring back
If I could I would peel off my skin
Let it fly away as light as a feather
There's no sanity left
To hold me together

You have dreams

You have lovers

You have it all in the palm of your hand

It's sweet and sour

You will strive, fall, and sometimes take a dive

But that's how you know

That you are truly alive

The stars are so shockingly bright at night
As they glow and take flight
They glide through my dreams as pure as can be
True as any eye can see
As I stare up at a map of darkness
The light warps together
I wish I could just stay here
For stars are like the truth
They show no lies, only proof
One day I will reach up and grab one
Bring it down
As its warmth touches my soul
I know I am found

I am stronger than I think
I know that now
I may get knocked down
But I will rise
After all, the moon becomes pieces every now and again
But full once more, it will continue to shine

Tell me a love story
Show me a princess trapped and broken
Who needs rescuing by a brave knight
Actually scratch that
Make it a dark knight
Who only knows the misfortunes of life
But believes he can redeem himself
And finally do something right
For the one he loves fully
Because change and transformation
Is the greatest love story

You are the light that shines the brightest
Not because you overshadow others in the room
But in the way you illuminate their very beings
Cores
Souls

Does age determine intelligence?
I feel that experience rivals all
Old or young, we grow

Moon and sun never meet
Lovers never sharing the same vast sky
Dark and light
Opposites attract

There was once a girl
Who made up her mind
She was going to be the best
Excel the most of her kind
She pushed herself hard
All for this one goal
It must've been quite the shock
When she learned she could fail and fall
You know what they say
Fall down seven times get up eight
However, the girl stumbled dozens
She refused the hard ground to be her fate
She had been taught to reach for the stars
She believed success was about the win
She didn't know the lesson would be so hard
So she fought it, kicked it, tried to cave it in
It took the girl many years
But one day she finally understood
As many wins you have in life, you also lose
You have to take the road less traveled
Or even forge one anew
The journey is yours, but it has its dips and turns
Most of all being the "best"
Is just the best version of you

Today I thought of you
Who am I kidding?
It happens all the time
Every hour
Minute
Second
Since I became yours
And you became mine

Do you ever notice the images of power and beauty
around you?
Thunder cracking
Lightning striking across the sky
Searing and splitting the stars apart
Wind forcing ancient trees to bend and bow to its will
Branches snapping
And leaves whirlwinding away
Wildfire sparks and ignites
A bright second of light
And life that captivates the eye
Before turning it all to ash
A dead whisper of smoke
Snowstorms howling with every gust and gale
A cold so fierce blocking out the enormity of the sun
Only to turn on its head
Settling into a crisp untouched wonderland
The first step outside in fresh snow

Discovering a new world
And then there's the rain
Pure and refreshing
It comes in drops and waves
Erasing the past, wiping your slate clean
The ultimate renewal
But only if you can survive its trial of
No air
All these acts of nature
That we fight and embrace at the same time
The power it holds
To give life and take it
Images that spark fear and ignite passion
It's devastatingly beautiful
So devastate me
Maybe I can feel beautiful too

Let me make something clear
No one wants to feel lost
No one asks to live in fear
When you try and pick up the pieces of me
It makes me feel more broken
I don't need you to understand
I don't need you to see
For the love of God, in these moments
Don't touch my skin
Caresses feel like broken glass
It's not going to heal me or let you in
I get that it hurts you deeply to see me this way
I feel your love and I know you want to help
But this isn't something that heals within a day
I won't lie
Sometimes it will be an inconvenience
I might not sleep and call you as late as 2 am
With nothing to say, only silence
I'm going to think physical pain is better
than mental agony
I'm going to slice and explore
I'll try to hide it and ignore your calls

I won't understand that I am scaring you shitless
Or that this will leave more permanent scars than the rest
The worst is when my temper will flare
I'll break a mirror or a plate, maybe two, maybe three
I'm going to snap like a wild animal
Not giving a damn or a fucking care
I'm going to lay in bed all day
Never turning on the lights
You will get worried
Finally impatient
We are going to have some pretty ugly fights
But if you stick it out I can promise you this
One day my smile will return and I will creep back
outside
I will laugh and hug again
I will be the girl you had really missed
I will still have many ups and downs
But I will learn to control them more
I just hope you realize that depression isn't one battle
But a lifelong war

Sitting in a garden
I whispered to the wind one night
"I wish to love another"
My voice was carried to the Heavens
And to my surprise
The goddesses peered down through the clouds at my little soul
They sung back into the starry air
"Little flower, before you can show your petals to the world, you must first bloom"
"Learn to love yourself before you give away your heart too soon"
Looking back, I should've heeded their warning
Instead I gave my love freely
Each person just took it and ran
Now instead of blooming petals
I'm just a flower pot filled with sand

He will compliment your soft lips
Try to undo every zipper and button
Say you have the most beautiful eyes
In order to access your curvy hips and thighs
But tell him it's not enough
Don't give in
Until he can match the intelligence of your mind

They look up at me with eyes of innocence
And hearts so pure
How do I tell them?
The world is not all they're hoping for

The power of wings
Is not in flight
But the ability
To lift others up

I traced my steps to see where I had been
But the only pattern I found
Was a line forward
And back again

Personal truth
Big dreams are much easier to grasp
The more callused your hands

Tell me your celestial sign
Mythology shows we are meant to be
The stars around us align

I want to get back
On this pedestal of mine
But it seems I've forgotten
How to climb

Generals of love only know the dirty tricks
They drill into us
"All is fair in love and war"
Neglecting to teach us the biggest step
How to say sorry
When you don't want to fight anymore

*

Why was I drawn to him?
At first I didn't know why myself
Maybe it was the moment my eyes found his
For that brief second he let me in
Just to shut me out again
And in that moment I saw
A beautifully complex person
I wonder if he saw his soul as cracked
Where I saw a beautiful tear that sheared the sky
That questioned the existence of the stars themselves
I wanted to sit next to him in the darkness
As he shared his sins
I wanted to walk with him in the fields where
he sowed his dreams
I wanted to watch him unravel at my fingers
As he lay completely raw before me
To be able to tell him
That he didn't need to put himself back together again
Hell, maybe in the beginning
I preferred his flaws over his perfections
Because maybe then I could rip this mask
off my face finally
The one that holds the fake smile
Of the girl who always pleases others
Maybe then, if I were with him
I could be completely human too

Remember you

Are a rose

In the garden of life

Darkness is fine

Its only once you've been buried that you can fully

bloom and see the light

Remember

The harder the rain falls the brighter your petals will be

It's life

Yes, people will look

So stand tall and leave them in awe

But if they try to touch

Remember you are a rose

Remember you have thorns

I need someone
With fire in their eyes
To match the storm in mine

88 . . .   THE DAY SHE LEARNED TO SPEAK

We were once butterflies
But society set the rules
Soon our creative wings were cut
Ingenuity
Distinction
Independence
Authenticity
Crumbled to dust
We laid them at our feet at dusk
Only to sit in chairs and stare at the sun
Count endless stars and envy floating clouds
Forgetting all we left behind
The day we gave up
Our right to fly

To survive as a lady
You must never stop learning
Obtain wisdom beyond your years
In order to question everything around you
Especially tales from liars' mouths
You must command attention like a proper queen
Dress as impeccably as a dowager
And in some situations
Swear like a sailor

All out of fight
During the darkest hour
She learned she could make her own light
She found how to stand with two legs
Yes, they were shaky at best
But from only knowing how to fall
And being forced to crawl
To now standing on her own two feet
Was no small feat

There are so many noises but not the one
I'm desperate to hear
Without it there's a void and it feels deadly silent
Wrong
I beg for answers
No one answers me as they talk to each other
"Not breathing"
I look up at the bright hospital lights
Then I'm gone
Here the lights are brighter and I see nothing but
silhouettes towering over me
But he's here
I can smell him
I can feel him without touching
My womb aches for him to come back
"Mine" I say weakly as I bleed from where they tore him
out of me
The silhouettes look down at me but don't hand him over
"Mine" my insides cry
"Mine" my heart screams
I grew him
I shared a body with him

I felt every kick, every bump
I sang and caressed and nurtured for months
I shared a heartbeat
And then I made a promise
I would walk
And when I couldn't walk I would drag my empty body
across the ground
I would find him over and over
I would never stop until he was in my arms
Because
Hell hath no fury
Like a mother
"Mine" I growl
And then the lights get too bright
And I blink
Back on the table
Cut wide open
Cold and shaking
But there it is
That sweet sound of a newborn's cry
Mine

The ink smudges
The paper tears
The tears fall
The heart beats
To write her story
Is what her soul truly needs
To write it down
When she can't say it out loud
Maybe someone far away
Or somewhere near
They will read these pages
They will feel her love
They will know
It's time to heal

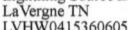

www.ingramcontent.com/pod-product-compliance
Lightning Source LLC
LaVergne TN
LVHW041536060526
838200LV00037B/1006